TAMSEN DONNER: A WOMAN'S JOURNEY

Tamsen Donner:
a woman's journey

by Ruth Whitman

with best wishes –

Ruth Whitman

ACKNOWLEDGMENTS

Some sections in this book first appeared in The Blacksmith;
in Discover America: Poems 1976 (*San Jose Studies*), *under
the title '*The Last Days of Tamsen Donner*'; and in* Ploughshares.
*A part of the Desert sequence won the John Masefield Award of
the Poetry Society of America.*

*I owe thanks to the National Endowment for the Arts for its
financial assistance, which made it possible for me to travel the
immigrant trail from Illinois to California; to the MacDowell
Colony for three hospitable summers during which this book was
written; and to the writings of John Bidwell, Myra Eells,
Narcissa Whitman, Patrick Breen, James Reed, Edwin Bryant,
Jesse Thornton, Francis Parkman, Mark Twain, George Stewart,
Bernard Devoto, and Wallace Stegner.* RW

Library of Congress Catalogue Card Number 77-90508
ISBN 0-914086-20-0
PRINTED IN THE UNITED STATES OF AMERICA
book designed by Bruce Chandler

cover photograph of an abandoned Conestoga wagon
from the *National Archives*

The publication of this book was supported by a grant from
the National Endowment for the Arts, Washington, D.C.,
and assisted by the Massachusetts Council on the Arts and
Humanities.

ALICE JAMES BOOKS
138 Mt. Auburn St.
Cambridge, Mass. 02138

CONTENTS

WHEN I began writing Tamsen Donner's lost journal, I did not know who I was writing about; only that I was writing in the person of a pioneer woman in the mid-nineteenth century, who was approaching a last range of mountains in the western part of the continent. When I finally identified her by name, I recognized her immediately, as though she were someone I had known.

Tamsen Donner was born in 1801 in Newburyport, Massachusetts. She was a teacher, wrote poetry, and had been married and widowed before she moved to Springfield, Illinois, where she met and married her second husband, George Donner.

Ten years later, in 1846, Tamsen and George decided to travel to California, where they could buy cheap land and where Tamsen planned to start a ladies' seminary. They traveled in style with their own three little girls and George Donner's two older daughters by a former marriage.

They planned the journey as a summer holiday, but it took months longer than they had anticipated. They followed an untraveled route across the Wasatch mountains. They miscalculated the time it would take to cross the Salt Desert. They lost animals, wagons, food. When they reached the Sierra, only a hundred miles from the Sacramento Valley, they were caught in a series of blizzards in one of the earliest and worst winters in western history. Snowed in for six months in the mountains, without provisions, many of the party resorted to cannibalism. Some of the children and the adults who could still walk were brought out by rescue parties. Tamsen refused to leave her husband, who was dying of an infected wound.

Tamsen had published poetry in the *Sangamon Journal* in Springfield and wrote a letter about the journey to her friend, Allen Francis, editor of the newspaper. But most of what she wrote — her diary, her poems, and all but three letters — has been lost.

In 1974 I followed her path along the Oregon and Mormon trails and along the Hastings cutoff across the Salt Desert to the Sierra mountains. During the trip I kept a journal, as I knew she had done. I discovered again — what I already knew — that in a poet's journal, prose passages become interlinked with lyrics, like recitative and aria, and these together help to weave back and forth between immediate and symbolic levels of reality.

Ruth Whitman
January, 1977

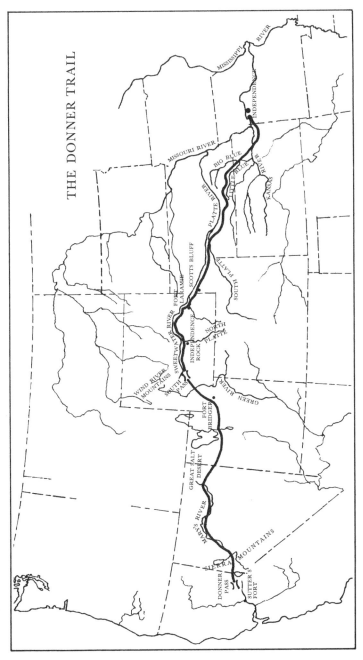

THE DONNER TRAIL

MISSISSIPPI RIVER

INDEPENDENCE

MISSOURI RIVER

BIG BLUE

LITTLE BLUE

KANSAS RIVER

PLATTE RIVER

SCOTTS BLUFF

SOUTH PLATTE

FORT LARAMIE

SWEETWATER RIVER

INDEPENDENCE ROCK

NORTH PLATTE

WIND RIVER MOUNTAINS

SOUTH PASS

GREEN RIVER

FORT BRIDGER

GREAT SALT DESERT

MARY'S RIVER

SIERRA MOUNTAINS

DONNER PASS

SUTTER'S FORT

Where is the West?
Who shall fix its limits?
He who attempts it will soon learn
that it is not a fixed but a floating line.

ELEUTHEROS COOKE, 1858

how could I foresee my end
in that soft Illinois spring?
I began my journey certain
that what was unknown
would be made smooth and easy

I forgot the anger of the land

now in the white silence I remember
wind blowing back the hair of the ocean
sunlight slicing through clouds
spring birds circling south

under the cities of snow
under the whirlpool of leaves
my beginning stirs again:
out of the white spring of my unbelief
a far blue country parts the sky

I   PRAIRIE

Westward Ho! For Oregon and California. Who wants to go to California without costing them anything? As many as eight young men, of good character, who can drive an ox team, will be accommodated by gentlemen who will leave this vicinity about the first of April. Come on Boys. You can have as much land as you want without costing you anything. The Government of California gives large tracts of land to persons who move there. The first suitable persons who apply will be engaged.
—GEORGE DONNER AND OTHERS.
The Sangamo Journal, March 26, 1846

Some are leaving this fall for Texas, and more are going in the spring to California and Oregon. For my part I have no desire to go anywhere. I am far enough west now and do believe some people might go west until they have been around the world and never find a place to stop.
—ELVIRA POWERS HYNES, in a letter to her sister, Illinois, March 1852

April 15, 1846, *leaving Springfield, Illinois.*

The wagons move first,
one directly behind the other,
but then straggling—
friends want to ride beside friends,
and we pass back and forth.
It is like a large summer party
      except for rumors that the Mormons
      who are also moving west this spring
      will massacre as many of us as they can;
      that the Indians will steal from anyone who
      separates from the train; that there may be
      war in California.
But we are surrounded by our friends
and at night outside the hollow square of wagons
we drown out the howling of the wolves
by singing hymns and old ballads around the campfires.

Just sometimes, when we are fairly on our way
one behind the other
undulating over the prairies
we have much the appearance
of a large funeral procession.

April 20, 1846, *on the Missouri prairie.*

The land flattens out most suddenly, long stretches of
flat fertile land, stands of young corn. The horizon is
everywhere. We picknicked by a huge flat field with a
sky broader and lower than ever in the East I could
imagine. Broad, low and blue, with herds of clouds.
The stretches themselves are punctuated here and
there with little isolated exclamation points — a house,
a barn, a shield of trees planted by an emigrant. Trees
show either that water is present or someone brought
a sapling to shade his house. Otherwise there are none.
Only immensity and loneliness. We change in relation
to the land. We become smaller.

May 11, 1846, *Independence, Missouri.*

My dear sister,
   *I commenced writing to you some months ago but the
letter was laid aside to be finished the next day and was never
touched. A nice piece of pink letter paper was taken out & now
has got so much soiled that it cannot be written upon & now
in the midst of preparation for starting across the mountains I
am seated on the grass in the midst of the tent to say a few
words to my dearest only sister. One would suppose that I
loved her but little or I should not have neglected her so long.*

*My three daughters are around me, one at my side trying to
sew, Georgeanna fixing herself in an old India rubber cap &
Eliza Poor knocking on my paper asking ever so many
questions. They often talk to me of Aunty Poor.*

*I can give you no idea of the hurry of this place. It is supposed
there be 7000 waggons start from this place this season. We
go to California to the bay of San Francisco. It is a four
months trip. We have three waggons furnished with food &
clothing drawn by three yoke of oxen each. We take cows along
and milk them & have some butter though not as much as we
would like. I am willing to go and have no doubt it will be an
advantage to our children and to us. I came here last evening
and start tomorrow morning on the long journey.*
              *Farewell my sister, you shall hear from
              me as soon as I have an opportunity*

        *Love to Mr. Poor the children
        & all friends   Farewell*
              T. E. Donner

May 26, 1846, *on the Kansas prairie.*

Where are the seagulls?

                crossing
the prairie, I keep mistaking hawks
for gulls: a thick wind
blows inside my head full of salt
and seafog

            now in my dreams I find
wild rosehips on the beach
at Newburyport: I'm a child
chasing waves across the sand
sails sting white against the blue

in these feathery seas of grass
traveling towards the steep
heart of America, why do I
keep watching for seagulls?

May 30, 1846, *along the Big Blue river.*

Talking to my friend, Mrs. Reed, who is fearful of the
journey and has a constant headache from the jolting
of the wagon, I see it is not with me as it is with the
other women. It is easier for me to change my life, to
think of a new kind of living.

As a girl I traveled from Newburyport in Massachusetts
to North Carolina to teach in the seminary in Elizabeth
City, and there at the age of twenty-eight I married
Tully Dozier and bore him two children, thinking this
would be my life forever. All three were taken from
me by fever in the space of two months.

My brother in Springfield asked me to come and take
care of his motherless children. So I began a new
second life. I journeyed for weeks in my grief, crossing
Massachusetts, going by waterway through New York,
by railway and coach through Pennsylvania and Ohio.
I found I had a taste for travel.

In Springfield, teaching my little scholars simple botany
in a farmer's field, I met George Donner, twice
widowed, who gave me my second family. He is a big
man, in soul as well as in body, and gives himself
freely to new things. So to sell our farm and pack up
our household for this journey seems to me not so
frightening. I carry my roots with me into a third life.
I am willing to make a home wherever we choose to
sleep.

June 2, 1846, *along the Big Blue.*

I find it awkward at first to bake out of doors but now
that I am becoming accustomed to it I do it quite
easily.

Our table is the ground,
our tablecloth an old India rubber spread,
our dishes of tin:

tin basins for tea cups,
iron spoons and plates
and several pans for milk

I find the wagon's jolting
can churn a pail of cream to butter
in a day's journey

June 8, 1846, *on the Platte river.*

Eliza follows a rabbit into some woods and brings me
back two enormous purple thistles and a cluster of
daisies. The fields along the river incredibly rich and
rolling. The immense sky full of gray clouds, mist, and
small rain.

> In the tangle beside a stream at noon
> we find large patches of strawberries
> wild and sweet and small wild roses
>
> slowly the clear sky of morning
> begins to breed thick clouds
>   until at sunset
> we are bathed in black and orange light
>
> we start down a road
> where the air hardly parts to let us through
> we are suddenly blinded by a rain
> that drenches our clothes, our wagon tops,
> our bedding
>
> but it is a small sparse rain after all
> not enough to fill the shallow river
> or moisten the ground

June 12, 1846, *on prairie creek.*

We dress in our night dresses for washing clothes, build a fire almost in the center of the creek on some stones, warm some water, and commence washing in the kettles as we have nothing else to supply the place of washtubs. We could get on well were the water soft, but that being hard, it takes all our strength and a great portion of our soap. Besides, our clothes will not look well, which spoils our anticipated merriment, but we find that we can heat water, wash, boil, and rinse in the same kettle.

One of the company brings us a little wild honey; we have a little sport with the fire running in the dead grass.

June 17, 1846, *on the North Platte.*

The morning is fierce with fresh smells:
prairie grass   clover   and the familiar
lupin paler than the sky bluer
than the periwinkle starring the ground
around the stream under willows and alders

I pick the wild blossom and mark the joining
of leaf to stem the design of
petal to petal
                    and I remember
the kiss of fingers
the joining   the holiday of eyes
in an Illinois meadow

                I had brought my class
                to study the wildflowers
                not knowing the tall farmer watching us
                owned the field and would be my future
                refuge

                a widow of thirty-five I had thought
                my body would not stir again
                my lifelong fires were banked
                but in his rich earth
                winter buds unclenched their tightness
                under his sun   his unaccustomed rain
                I shed my widowhood
                and let a new self burgeon

husbanded again have I finally learned
to let be let go? the need
to find oneself within a man
is not so great the second time

but we are like two voices of a strain
that come together and go apart
each echoing but singing independently
knowing the coming together in the end
    will thread into a single theme

June 18, 1846, *along the Platte.*

We watch the land dry out. Trees grow smaller and
disappear. Patches of light sand, and then, on the
plains, long low hills. We keep crossing and recrossing
the Platte,—ugly, shallow, and as the mountain men
say, a mile wide and a foot deep.

We pass a dead ox and two graves of children.

> We sometimes see
> the shattered wrecks
> of ancient clawfooted
> tables, well waxed and rubbed
> or massive bureaus of carved oak
> sitting along the track:
> once loved relics
> flung out
> to scorch and crack
> on the hot prairie

June 21, 1846, *near Ash Hollow.*

Strange moundlike formations begin to appear out of the dry flat bottoms. At Ash Hollow we are obliged to pull our wagons and oxen over the high ledge with ropes and pulleys. George and the men work well together and we are able to pass through without damage.

There are strange alkali smells from the surrounding earth. The land is powdered with traces of white sour salt. The sparse water poisons the cattle. Many of the families are constantly sick with dysentery. So far our little ones have been spared that misery.

June 25, 1846, *on the Laramie plains.*

We creep along the Platte
in shifting sands and quicksands

the dusty earth is covered with a salt
so poisonous it spoils the springs

my woolen skirt is stained
my shawl is torn from catching

sharp corners in our crowded wagon
my bonnet is limp from sudden rains

rising ahead in the flat valley
a monstrous chimney

towers like an obelisk:
ruins and castles

turrets knobs violent peaks
like shapes our children see

when they awaken frightened in the night
and here I find among these monuments

a cactus shape
                low to the ground

with ears and spines and a sudden flower
like a giant buttercup above

the green:
                    a smile of yellow in a twisted land

July 4, 1846, *at Fort Laramie.*

Dressed in our best clothes, which we have saved for this occasion, we come together in a grove and open the bottle of wine our old friends in Springfield gave us. They promised they would toast us today, facing towards the west, as we drink to them, lifting our glasses to the east.

> So do we make a link
> between what we were
> and what we have become:
>
> we are inventing
> the body of a land
> binding together
>
> two halves of a whole
> as we touch each other
> across a thousand miles
>
> and I who started
> a thousand miles before
> feel in my flesh
>
> the stretch of the land
> as we give it birth
> the long spill of it
> unrolling before us

July 12, 1846, *near Independence rock.*

At night when the fires have died I think of my New England, which now seems tiny and cramped compared to the enormous spaces we are living in. We are watching Laramie peak ahead, sprinkled with snow like confectioner's sugar. The ground is cracked, baked, covered with colonies of small sage brush. We stop at the Rock and read the travelers' names scratched there, despite the brutal mosquitoes that aim for scalp and ears. But that is no worse than the hot wind that blows perpetually, covering us with bitter dust.

   Sage brush:
   a two-foot tree
   with rough bark spiny foliage twisted boughs
   a delicate graygreen spreading its tint
   over hill and desert:

   smells like our herb
   but sharp as turpentine
   pungent in campfires
   hardy:

   in deep sand among barren rocks
   everywhere peopling the peopleless spaces
   like us
   where nothing else in the world would grow

July 15, 1846, *near the end of the North Platte river.*

Moving down-sun
I learn to read water
by willows and alders:

a line of cottonwoods,
a green stripe across a desert,
scrubby cedars on a hillside

signal a spring in a gully:
pines on a mountain
announce a running stream:

moving down-sun
our water has been rank
men and oxen are sick with it

but now in the unexpectable land
we come to an untainted stream
cold and fresh Sweet Water

most beautiful of names
the last stream
on the eastern side of the mountains

as we start to climb
there leaps out of the distance
north of west

a city
of stony mountains
under a roof of perpetual snow

the first snow I have ever seen in summer

July 18, 1846, *crossing the Great Divide.*

An end or a beginning:
is this the place where being separates
from itself the precise moment
the space between pulse and pulse

at one instant we are moving towards:
transporting the furniture of our lives
bringing the particularities of one existence
to an imagined point where we are taken in
formalized justified like an embrace
without an end

but no love is so final   merely
having traced ourselves back to our
Atlantic beginnings
we change from source to source
leap to a new love plunging westward
where once we looked backward all the way

now hesitant among the mountains
we pass across the invisible boundary
that divides self from self
and move forward heartlong towards the other sea
a twin
a mirror of ourselves

II   DESERT

The most direct route, for the California emigrants, would be to leave the Oregon route, about two hundred miles east from Fort Hall; thence bearing west southwest, to the Salt Lake; and thence continuing down to the bay of San Francisco.
— LANSFORD HASTINGS, The Emigrants'
Guide to Oregon and California, 1845

The Californians were generally much elated and in fine spirits, with the prospect of a better and nearer road to the country of their destination. Mrs. George Donner was, however, an exception. She was gloomy, sad, and dispirited, in view of the fact that her husband and others could think for a moment of leaving the old road and confide in the statements of a man about whom they knew nothing but who was probably some selfish adventurer. Mercury at sunrise 46°; sunset 52°.
— JESSE QUINN THORNTON, Oregon and
California, 1849.

July 21, 1846, *on Little Sandy creek.*

As we come down the western side of the Divide we
find patches of purple flowers and orange daisies. But
the country is still windy, dry, uninhabited, and the
children are beginning to tire. The wagons too are
aging more rapidly than we expected and must be
tarred constantly. But George remains his cheerful self
and talks continually of that wonderful California land
where it is always spring. I wonder what flowers would
bloom perpetually.

> Tumbleweed:
> a densely branched spherical
> Amaranthus plant
>   withered   broken off
> and rolling wildly across the plains
> in the wind
>   or huddled together
> against the wagons
> clasped in each other's spiny arms
>
> the children chase the bristly creatures
> as though they were chasing
> hoops or balls
>
> the rootless chasing the rootless

July 25, 1846, *along the Big Sandy.*

Thus we scatter as we go along
the arid stretches are so dry
the hills are so steep
that we must constantly tar
and mend the wheels

it would have been better
not to bring
any baggage whatever
only what is necessary
to use on the way

if I were to make this journey again
I would make quite different preparations
    to pack and unpack so many times
    and cross so many streams

the custom of the mountain men
is to possess nothing
and then you will lose nothing

July 27, 1846, *on the way to Green river.*

A white blindness of salts:
it makes us squint
it glares like snowfields under the sun
it glimmers and quivers in snaky heat waves
our hair clothing wagons
covered with white dust
we cannot stop to wash away

the children complain
of grit in their mouths
as we pass plains filled with shimmering lakes
that quench no thirst

July 28, 1846, *at Fort Bridger.*

After miles of brown-gray hills and buff-colored deserts,
Fort Bridger appears wonderfully green, with rushing
brooks and groves of trembling aspen. It eases our
thirst just to look at the trees.

There has been a change of plan. A Mr. Lansford
Hastings has sent us a letter from Sweetwater promising
to meet us here and guide us across a shorter route to
California. But he is not here.

It is a two-hundred-mile cutoff around the Great Salt
Lake and across a small salt desert. George and Jim
Reed are eager to try it, and Mr. Bridger encourages
them, but Joe Walker, the mountain man, cautions us
against it since there is no clear trail.

My heart misgives me. We are all weary, many of us
are sick. In a month summer will be over. Our supplies
diminish. How can we trust an absent guide?

August 14, 1846, *crossing the Wasatch mountains.*

We are traveling blind.

   The trail thins and disappears
                            diminished
   like a river to a stream the stream snakes down
   to a trickle in the ground

   we age in the youngest canyon and still we climb
   carving out on the steepest ridge
   an inch-long place

   chaos of brush and boulders
   tangles of cottonwood and willow
                          we fumble through
   the same unpassable passage
   our days become
   like cliffs   around   around

   we are playing blindman's buff, hands outstretched:
   we are children in the dark who cannot find
   one mapped familiar face

August 27, 1846, *near the Salt Lake.*

It has taken us twenty-one days to go thirty-six miles, wandering through blind canyons, long ascents, narrow defiles choked with brush. We finally come down the ten-mile descent into this lovely valley circled by snowy mountains. If I were leading the emigrants, I would be tempted to settle and build a new city here.

August 28, 1846, *in the Salt Lake Valley.*

Here in the cracked earth
twenty deep pools:
pure eyes from another world
without salt or alkali
each spring so bewitched
that when you dip water
out of the smallest or the greatest
it comes filling back to the brim
not flowing over
not an inch below the lip
but inexhaustible

is it a sign
as in the fairy tale
that charity
            that love
will not go dry?

September 1, 1846, *at the edge of the Salt Desert.*

We find scraps of paper with bits of handwriting
scattered on the ground at the foot of a post. Perhaps
it is a message for us.

Spread on my lap where I
have gathered blossoms, held
my babies, I hold this
future:
random shreds of paper
have a scheme the listening
hand the patient hand must
find.
I ask the angles
where they want to go. The
pattern is all in the
being.
And I am the
instrument to find their
form, as the hazel wand
finds water:

hard drive   two
days and nights
no water

September 5, 1846, *in the Salt Desert.*

After three days and nights in this desert of salt I am
obliged to give the children little cubes of sugar to
suck on, to ease their thirst, and flattened bullets to
chew on, to keep their juices flowing. Finally, in the
cold night, we sleep. Towards dawn with a mouth dry
as paper, I dream of a morning rain storm:

> That gray satin quilt the ocean
> is ruffled by first rain
>
> sterling arrows fall on it
> iron muscles underneath the quilt
>
> loll and flinch, unwilling to combine:
> pour sky and become ocean
>
> let the steel drumbeats celebrate
> the yielding beast the mixing elements
>
> let gray behemoths of rain
> enter and flood my valleys

September 6, 1846, *in the desert.*

Go light go light I must walk lightly

as I moved from one life to another
more and more followed me:
gowns books furniture
paints notebooks

now the seven of us — even the little girls —
must have substance
to carry into the new country

we are transporting a houseful:
barrels of flour stuffed with porcelain
pots tin plates silver service quilts
salt meat rice sugar dried fruit
coffee tea
              the wagon sags
and the oxen falter
                        one wagon founders

what shall I let go? books:
                              the least
needed for survival: in the cold
desert night
              George lifts my heavy
crate of Shakespeare, Emerson, Gray's
Botany, spellers and readers for my school

and hides it in a hill of salt
while the children sleep parched
and the cows and oxen stand mourning:
I put aside my desk with the inlaid pearl
our great fourposter with the pineapple posts
my love my study

what else can I part with?
I will keep one sketchbook one journal
to see me to the end of the journey

go light
go light
I must walk lightly

September 7, 1846, *in the desert.*

Across the white plain of salt
I see an army of wagons
teams dogs children
passing near the horizon
and rejoice to think
another company
is breaking way for us
heading towards the water

and I see a woman:
long skirted in a bonnet
and beside her another woman
multiplied twenty times
who turns who stops
begins again even as I
turn stop begin
and then I understand

how the need for another being
is turned back on oneself
even as rays of heat
turn back and curve upward
against the reflected image

we discover we are traveling
beside no one
but ourselves

September 25, 1846, *near Marys river.*

We are facing
the last mountains:
sometimes we walk
with the children
beside the wagon
to rest the lame oxen

the mountains rise
unscalable
the road is
a fiction
I am not inside this story
I am sitting
beside my husband
a frame
to the picture

there is surf I know
on the other side of the pass:
somewhere beyond this wall
the end of land
and a summer sea

III   MOUNTAIN

. . . here I met Mrs. Reed and two children two still in the mountains, I cannot describe the death like look they all had Bread Bread Bread Bread was the beging of every child and grown person except my wife I give to all what I dared and left for the scene of desolation and now I am camped within 25 miles which I hope to mak this night and tomorrow we had to camp soon on account of the softness of the snow, the men falling in to their middles.

—James Reed's diary, Feb. 26, 1847

. . . O Mary I have not rote you half of the truble we have had but I have rote you anuf to let you now that you dont now what truble is   but thank god we have all got throw and the onely family that did not eat human flesh   we have left everything but i dont cair for that   we have got throw with our lives but Dont let this letter dishaten anybody   never take no cutofs and hury along as fast as you can

—twelve-year-old Patty Reed's letter
to her cousin, May 16, 1847

55

October 12, 1846, *near Truckee meadows.*

There was a film of ice on the bucket of water this morning.

We followed Marys river until it disappeared into the ground. But we are no longer surprised at distortions of nature.

Now after traveling across another miserable alkali desert, through dusty hills and dry miles, we come to these green meadows. We will stay to replenish ourselves and our oxen. We are tired and disorganized almost beyond repair.

October 28, 1846, *on the Truckee river.*

Straining downhill
our axle breaks
the wagon falls
to one side but
George scoops out the
sleeping children

he starts to cut
a piece of wood
to mend the break
the chisel carves
an angry gash
across his hand

It is starting to snow.

November 3, 1846, *by Alder creek.*

Stopped.
    We can go no further.
Here steep in the mountains
the flakes thicken down
heavier and heavier
the white veils swirl between us
and the pass

George with his injured hand
starts to fell the trees
to build a shelter
but the snow falls and falls
fat flakes
sent to wind us in a
thick sheet
we have no time to pitch a tent
we make a shed of brush
roughed over with pine boughs
rubber coats blankets and skins
the two little ones sit on a log
snug in a buffalo robe
cheerfully watching us work
thinking it fun to catch the snow
on their tongues

inside this strange
dwelling place
I must build a fire
and make another nest

November 8, 1846, *by Alder creek.*

Storms hammer us:
snow covers our shelter,
our wagons, oxen alive and dead

we cut steps upward
to get to the light
watch westward over the crest

for help: no one comes

looking for food
George has shot
a coyote, an owl,

a wounded bear:
not food enough
to cure our hunger

November 12, 1846, *by Alder creek.*

The wound on George's hand does not heal. He feels
ill and cannot stand up, although he protests it is
nothing and will pass. The poison seems to be traveling
up his arm to his shoulder. I bathe it in melted snow,
salve it, bind it up, assuring him with all my love that
it will improve. But it worsens. I think it begins to
smell of decay, although it is hard to distinguish smells,
we have lived so long in this close wet space.

The children were glad at first to stop in one place
and play in the snow, but now they prefer to lie quietly
in bed, keeping each other warm.

So it falls to me to fetch twigs for the fire, prepare our
little food, and make the time pass until help comes. I
have told all the stories I can remember and sung all
the songs.

November 25, 1846, *by Alder creek.*

When I look at this strong man
lying injured on his bed of boughs
or watch him sleeping vulnerable

I remember him
as a motherless boy:
what makes the ordinary features

of an ordinary man
suddenly uncommon
or the events of a usual life

mythical and rare:
I think of him as a boy of eight
sent out into the fields to play

in clean new overalls:
and the skunk he met
braver than he   who baptised him

with its generous stink
and the farmer's wife
who buried his shoes

and his spoiled brandnew overalls:
how ashamed he was
the frightened boy

now my tidy husband elegant
and courteous
even in his pain

lying here with his festering wound

December 5, 1846, *by Alder creek.*

All the oxen and cows that were alive are dead and lost beyond recovery under the snow. Fires are unsafe, all water frozen, and the light shut out. I still have some tea and sugar left, and a few hides from the cattle. The thousand dollars sewn up in the quilt that covers the children is nothing but dead paper to us.

We hear that a party from the other camp at the Lake is attempting to walk out on snowshoes made of split oxbows and strips of hide to get help from Sutter's Fort in Sacramento.

December 26, 1846, *by Alder creek.*

I have come up out of our black hole beneath the snow
(where the children sleep all day in damp clothing
and George lies without stirring)
to breathe the sharp white air

these mountains
comfort me
a blazing army
straddling the sky
with their long pyramidal pines
dark green black green
trees trees a profusion of trees at last
against the emerald lake

these shapes these colors cleanse my eyes
and I turn back to our evil-smelling cave
a little stronger to confront
the next meal and the next day and the next

January 7, 1847, *by Alder creek.*

I thought of mother's bread, as a child would, but did
not find it on the table.

> The field mice
> that creep into the camp
> we catch and use
> to ease the pangs of hunger
> pieces of hide
> we cut in strips
> singe scrape and boil
> to glue: hard-to-swallow
> marrowless bones
> boiled and scraped
> we burn and eat
> we chew the bark
> and twigs of pine
> to keep from crying
> for meat and bread

February 19, 1847, *by Alder creek.*

There is no choice. We have somehow survived these months in our dark hole under twenty feet of snow with nothing to fill us but gristle and dried buffalo hide, but now I must send George's two older girls with the kind men who have come to lead them over the pass to Sutter's Fort and California.

Many have died of hunger, of cold, of despair. And I am not sure, with only a few skins left, how long we can keep from eating the bodies of our dead as others are doing.

George begs me to go with the children, but I can not, I will not leave him to die without my comfort.

March 1, 1847, *by Alder creek.*

Must we devour ourselves
in order to survive?

    is this new continent
    a place where we can live

only by thrusting down
that fragile barrier

    the ancient loathing
    to eat each other's flesh?

for my children I find it
not so hard:

    I must give them
    nourishment

from whatever source
they will not question where

    but for me
    I cannot see

how I could bear to live
by eating my friend's death

March 15, 1847, *by Alder creek.*

I send my three little ones away with the second
rescue party. I dress them in layers of their best clothes
and tell them to be sure to say to everyone they meet
that they are the children of George Donner. I take
them to the other camp, kiss them each, and beg them
not to cry. I walk back alone to our empty nest.

> My children move in my mind
> like miniatures
> painted on ivory:
> one light and willowy
> one rosy dark
> and the littlest
> a frisky animal
> that refuses to be tamed:
> she reaches through the frame
> and pulls at my skin
> a baby sloth
> clutching its mother's fur
>
> I etch them in my brain
> like diamond scratches on a windowpane:
> arrest their images as though I were
> a limner passing through, a peddler
> of portraits

April 10, 1847, *by Alder creek.*

How can I store against coming loss?
what faculties of the heart
can I bring against this parting?

we traveled across the land
towards winter not towards spring

I watched the children become solemn and thin
our wagons and housewares
brittle
            depleted

when I buried my boxes
my watercolors and oils my writing desk

I felt I had given all I could part with:
that was what the desert demanded of me:
then the canyons and boulders

ate at the wheels of our wagons
squeezed the life from our oxen

and we learned to part from our
livestock our friends
our comfort

how can I part with
my sustaining love
who was father

to the whole camp, orphans and families
who whistled us up at dawn

who nooned me in the shade
and fed me at sunset
the darks and lights of his eyes

playing over me like sun and clouds
on a highhearted summer afternoon:

how can I learn to sleep
without his shoulder
to bed down my griefs?

the sun stays hidden
for months the sky has wept its snow

April 12, 1847, *Alder creek.*

Hunger. The lightness of it. I feel my legs will not
hold me up any longer. Sounds enter the senses
sharply, colors are very bright, I am filled with light,
a music that the saints sought and called God. I am
not quite in touch with the ground, I am outside my
own body. It would be easy to join the air and float
into nothingness.

April 15, 1847, *in the mountains.*

Cobblestones of light
have poured my path
east to west:
the gull swoops
in the low tide
leaving little crab claws
washed out pink
where the atlantic sun
sucked out the quick

From notes by Thomas Fallon, leader of the final
salvage expedition to Donner Lake:

books calicoes tea
coffee shoes percussion caps
household and kitchen furniture
are scattered about

the body of George Donner
is carefully wrapped
in a large clean white sheet
in the midst of filth

Mrs. Donner's body
is nowhere to be found

If my boundary stops here
I have daughters to draw new maps on the world
they will draw the lines of my face
they will draw with my gestures my voice
they will speak my words thinking they have invented
                them

they will invent them
they will invent me
I will be planted again and again
I will wake in the eyes of their children's children
they will speak my words